Contents

Growing up 4

Agnes changes her name 6

Poor people in India 8

Teresa leaves the convent 10

Mother Teresa shows she's right 12

The Missionaries of Charity 14

Children are a gift from God 16

Helping the sick 18

Famous 20

A timeline of Mother Teresa's life 22

Index 24

More books to read 24

Growing up

Mr and Mrs Bojaxhiu lived in Albania. In 1910, their daughter Agnes was born which made them very happy. Now they had three children: two girls and one boy. All the children did well at school and had lots of friends. The family often went to the local Catholic church.

Famous People

Mother Teresa
1910–1997

Sydney Wood

Sydney Wood has written numerous history books for primary and secondary schools, as well as books and articles for adults. He is a former senior lecturer in history and is actively involved in curriculum development.

Picture credits

Hulton Getty: pages 9, 11, 20

Topham Picturepoint: pages 17, 19

Published by 4Learning

124 Horseferry Road

London

SW1P 2TX

Written by Sydney Wood
Edited by Anne Fleck and Jackie Mace
Illustrated by Gary Wing
Picture research by ilumi
Designed by HA Design
Printed by ESP Colour
ISBN 186215 8584

For further information about 4Learning and
details of published materials, e-mail
4learning.info@channel4.co.uk

www.channel4.com/learning

Mr Bojaxhiu died when Agnes was just eight. Her mother had to work hard to earn money for the family. She was always very kind to people who were poor or sick, even though she did not have much money.

Mother, I must give my life to God. I must leave home and train to be a nun. Then I must work in India.

Agnes had heard about India from her local Catholic priest. Priests from Albania worked in India and wrote home. In the letters they explained how much the people in India needed help.

Agnes had chosen to become a nun. Nuns lived in special buildings called convents. Here they prayed. They read the Bible and other religious books. They went to church services every day and promised to obey the Church's rules. They promised never to marry. They also promised not to own jewels, lots of clothes and other things.

When Agnes was 18 years old she left home. She joined a group of nuns called the Sisters of Loreto who worked in India. There they ran schools for Indian children in their convents. But first Agnes had to begin her training as a nun.

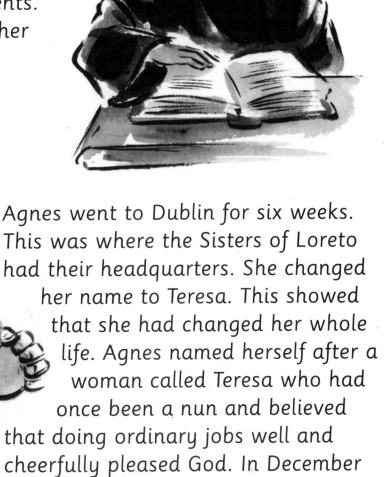

Agnes went to Dublin for six weeks. This was where the Sisters of Loreto had their headquarters. She changed her name to Teresa. This showed that she had changed her whole life. Agnes named herself after a woman called Teresa who had once been a nun and believed that doing ordinary jobs well and cheerfully pleased God. In December 1928, Teresa set off for India.

Poor people in India

Teresa began teaching in Darjeeling in India. Two years later she was sent to a convent in Calcutta. Over six million people lived in this city, but there were not enough homes for all of them. In 1941, a war began between the Japanese and the British, who ruled India. Sometimes the Japanese bombed Calcutta. This war ended in 1945 only for new trouble to begin. The British left India. Following this, there was terrible fighting between Indians who believed in different religions.

Thousands died and India split into two countries – India and Pakistan.

There were so many people in Calcutta that at least 200,000 did not have homes. They lived on the streets. They did not have proper food or water. Some starved and became weak and ill. Hospitals did not have room for street people who became ill. Children grew up without any education.

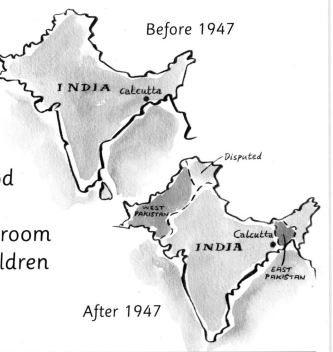

Before 1947

After 1947

I have never seen so many poor people. How can I help them?

The people of Calcutta were very poor.

Teresa spent several years teaching in the convent school in Calcutta. In 1937, she was put in charge of it. In this year she finished her training as a nun. Now she was called 'Mother', not 'Sister', Teresa.

There were times when Mother Teresa left the convent. She saw many very poor people. One day in 1946 she saw many dead bodies in the streets. Over 5,000 people had been killed in Calcutta due to fighting between Indians of different religions. Such sights troubled Teresa. On 10 September 1946 she heard God telling her she must really help the poor. But first the Church had to allow her to go.

May I leave? I must go and live with the poorest people and help them.

I will talk to the Archbishop. You must not rush into this.

The Archbishop let Teresa leave the convent for one year only. She had to prove that she really could help the very poor by living with them. She left the convent on 16 August 1948, although she was still a nun. She now wore a white sari like those worn by Indian women. Mother Teresa had to learn how to care for the sick properly. She spent four months with nuns who were experts in medical care.

Mother Teresa began working with the poor people of Calcutta. All she had were her sandals, her clothes and a few coins given to her by the Archbishop.

Mother Teresa in her white sari and sandals.

Mother Teresa shows she's right

Teresa went to work in Motijhil, one of the very poorest parts of Calcutta. She had to show the Archbishop she could really help people by sharing their lives. But she had no money, nowhere to live and no one to help her.

In March 1949, a girl from a rich family came to her. She had been one of Teresa's pupils. Now she began to work with Teresa. She took the name Sister Agnes. Other girls joined her, so Teresa was no longer alone.

Teresa and her helpers begged for food and medicines from people who could afford to give them. Some rich people gave them money too. One such person was Michael Gomes. He offered Mother Teresa and her helpers a whole floor of his house to live in. He did not ask for any money for this.

Teresa started a school. At first she had to teach the alphabet by scratching letters in the earth. Then people gave her furniture and a blackboard.

Teresa and her helpers comforted poor people dying on the streets. They cleaned them and talked to them.

They saved people who were sick or starving. They found many of these people lying in the big railway stations.

After a year the Archbishop saw how much good Teresa was doing. He allowed her group to become a proper church group called 'The Missionaries of Charity'. The Pope then agreed that groups like this could be set up in other places.

The Missionaries of Charity

More young women joined Mother Teresa. By 1953 they had to move to a bigger house. It was named 'the Mother House'. It is still the headquarters of the Missionaries of Charity today.

Any woman who joined the Missionaries to train to become a Sister had to give up all she owned. The Sisters lived hard lives.

A Sister's day

 4:40am. The Sisters get up and wash in buckets of cold water. Each Sister has three saris and two lots of underclothes. Clothes must be washed in buckets. The Sisters wear sandals. Mother Teresa makes sure everyone eats breakfast.

🕕 6:00am. There are prayers and a religious service.

🕢 7:45am. The Sisters go out to work in twos. They carry all they need in bags. If it is raining, they can borrow umbrellas.

🕛 Midday. Time to return for something to eat. There are prayers and half an hour's rest, too.

🕑 2:00pm. The Sisters go back to work among the poorest people and the dirtiest streets.

🕕 6:00pm. Time to return for a meal. There are prayers and a religious service. There is time to read the Bible and other religious books. There are clothes to mend and house cleaning to do. Then there is time to talk about the day.

🕙 10:00pm. Bedtime.

Mother Teresa would not allow anything to be wasted. Even underclothes were often made from sacks. In 1963, a group of men began to live the same sort of lives. They called themselves 'The Missionary Brothers of Charity'.

Children are a gift from God

Mother Teresa loved children, but some Calcutta parents were too poor to feed their new babies. Sometimes they left them in doorways or dustbins. Other children were alone because their parents had died. Children like these had to live by begging. They often became very ill.

Mother Teresa managed to get Dr Roy, who was in the local government, to help her. A home for children called 'Shishu Bavan' was set up. The Sisters welcomed every child and baby brought there. All were washed, dressed properly, fed and loved.

Every child matters to God. We must do our best to love and care for these poor children.

The Sisters ran schools. They taught children to read and write. Sometimes rich people gave the Sisters money to send poor children to schools that could teach them extra skills to help them get jobs.

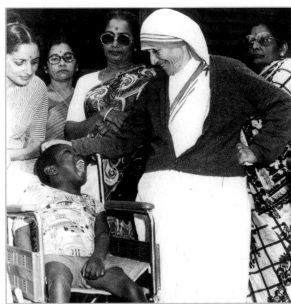

Mother Teresa cared for sick children.

Some children were adopted by families in India or other countries. Some were able to go back to their parents.

Helping the sick

Many people in Calcutta became ill because they did not have enough food. Starving people came into the city when their farms were hit by floods or other problems. The Missionaries of Charity did their best to feed these people.

Mother Teresa never gave up. She even took sick people to hospital in a wheelbarrow if there was no other way. She was particularly keen to find ways of helping those with a terrible illness called leprosy. She set up centres to treat them and worked hard to build a special village for them.

One day, Mother Teresa found a woman by the roadside. She was dying. She was so weak she could not stop rats from attacking her. Mother Teresa carried the woman to hospital and would not leave until a bed was found.

Mother Teresa asked the government for an empty building to use for dying people. She was given one that was very dirty. The Sisters cleaned it and laid out mattresses in it. Here they washed, fed and cared for dying people who had no one to look after them.

The Missionaries of Charity fed and clothed people.

Mother Teresa's work made her famous. Hundreds of young women joined the Missionaries of Charity. New centres for their work opened all over India. Important people came to see her. Gifts of money arrived. People in other countries collected clothes and medicines for her. In 1965, the Pope allowed her to open centres in other countries, too. In 1971, he gave her his Prize for Peace.

Mother Teresa was given many awards. Here she is in 1979 holding the Nobel Prize for Peace.

Queen Elizabeth visited India in 1983. She gave Mother Teresa the Order of Merit.

Mother Teresa received the Nobel Prize for Peace.

Mother Teresa travelled all over the world. She visited the Missionaries in other countries and asked rich people for help. But India was the country that she loved best.

In 1997 Mother Teresa died. She had always worked very hard. Sometimes she had been very ill. Today, her work continues all over the world. She will always be remembered for her strong religious belief that led her to give her whole life to serving the poorest and most lonely people.

A timeline of Mother Teresa's life

Agnes
Bojaxhiu
was born
in Albania

Agnes took
the name
Teresa

Teresa
began
teaching in
Darjeeling
in India

Teresa
made her
final
promises
to be
a nun

In the year

1910   1928   1929   1937

                1928   1931   1937   1946

Teresa left
Albania to
become a
nun

Teresa
began
teaching in
Calcutta

Teresa
became
head of
her school

Terrible
fighting
split India
into two
countries

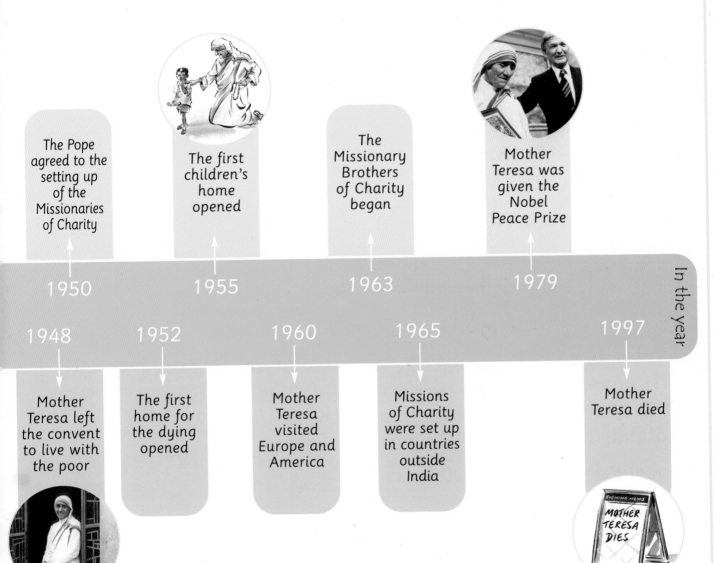

The Pope agreed to the setting up of the Missionaries of Charity

The first children's home opened

The Missionary Brothers of Charity began

Mother Teresa was given the Nobel Peace Prize

In the year

1950   1955   1963   1979

1948   1952   1960   1965   1997

Mother Teresa left the convent to live with the poor

The first home for the dying opened

Mother Teresa visited Europe and America

Missions of Charity were set up in countries outside India

Mother Teresa died

Index

Albania; 4–5
Archbishop; 10–11, 13

Bojaxhiu, Mr and Mrs
(Mother Teresa's parents); 4

Calcutta; 8–10, 18
Convents; 6, 10

Gomes, Michael; 12

India; 7–9, 17, 20–21

Leprosy; 18

Missionaries of Charity;
13–14, 18, 20
Missionary Brothers of
Charity; 15
Motijhil; 12

Nobel Prize for Peace; 20
Nuns; 6–7, 11

Order of Merit; 20

Shishu Bavan; 16
Sisters of Loreto; 7

More books to read

Mother Teresa
by Charlotte Gray
(Exley, 1988)

*Mother Teresa,
An Authorised Biography*
by Katherine Spink
(Fount, 1997)

My Life for the Poor
by Mother Teresa
(Harper and Row, 1985)